iOS 17 USER GUIDE

"Mastering iOS 17 with Your Definitive User Guide"

By

Gen Scott

TABLE OF CONTENTS

1 . Introduction
- Advantages of using the new iOS 17

2 . Chapter 1: Get Started
- Set up your iPhone
- Learn the basics of iOS
- Personalize your iPhone

3 . Chapter 2: Communication
- Phone calls
- FaceTime
- Messages
- Mail

4 . Chapter 3: Photos and Camera
- Take photos and videos
- Edit photos and videos
- Share photos and videos

5 . Chapter 4: iCloud
- IOS 17 upgrades for icloud

6 . Chapter 5: Accessibility
- Accessibility features on iPhone
- Turn on accessibility features

7 . Chapter 6 : Troubleshooting

- Common problems and solutions

- Get support from Apple
- Features and tricks
- iOS 17 specifications

8 . Conclusion

INTRODUCTION

Welcome to the iOS 17 User Guide, your comprehensive companion to the latest iteration of Apple's mobile operating system. iOS 17 is here to elevate your iPhone and iPad experience, introducing a host of exciting features and enhancements aimed at making your devices more productive, enjoyable, and user-friendly.

In this user guide, we'll embark on a journey through the most prominent additions to iOS 17, offering insights, tips, and tricks to help you make the most of these innovations. Whether you're a seasoned Apple aficionado or a newcomer to the iOS ecosystem, there's something valuable waiting for you in these pages.

Discover iOS 17's game-changing features, including:

- StandBy: Transform your iPhone into a dynamic smart display while it's charging, unlocking new possibilities.
- Live Activities in full screen: Stay up-to-date with real-time updates, whether it's sports scores or food delivery progress.
- Siri results at a glance: Siri's enhanced visual results provide a richer experience that's easily accessible.

- Visual Look Up: Uncover the hidden world within your photos and videos, from finding recipes to identifying objects and landmarks.
- Home: A revamped Home architecture promises improved performance and reliability.
- FaceTime: Enjoy Live Captions during FaceTime calls, capture Live Photos, and explore other enhancements.

Plus, delve into other noteworthy features like improved autocorrect, refreshed AirDrop, voicemail on FaceTime, and more.

Getting started with iOS 17 is a breeze. You can update your device over the air or connect to a computer and use iTunes or Finder for a seamless upgrade.

Once you're on iOS 17, we'll guide you through essential tips and shortcuts to maximize your experience:

- Easily access StandBy by positioning your charging iPhone sideways.
- Swipe down from the top right corner for full-screen Live Activities.
- Elevate your Siri interactions by simply lifting your iPhone to eye level.
- Dive into Visual Look Up by tapping and holding a subject in photos or videos.

- Embrace the improved Home architecture via the Home app's addition button.
- Engage Live Captions during FaceTime calls and capture memorable moments with Live Photos.

These highlights only scratch the surface of iOS 17's potential. Our guide covers these features in detail and more, ensuring you're well-equipped to navigate the iOS 17 landscape.

As you explore iOS 17's capabilities, remember that this guide is your trusty companion. It's designed to empower you with insights and instructions, making your iOS journey both enjoyable and efficient.

Let's embark on this exciting iOS 17 adventure together. Whether you're upgrading for productivity, entertainment, or simply the joy of discovering something new, iOS 17 has something remarkable in store for you."

Advantages Of Using The New Ios 17

IOS 17 is the latest version of Apple's mobile operating system, and it comes with a number of new features and benefits. Here are some of the main advantages of iOS 17

1 . Improved security and privacy

Lock Screen notifications that are only visible to you: This means that only you will be able to see the content of your notifications when your iPhone is locked. This is helpful for protecting your privacy in public places.

Better control over who can see your location: iOS 17 gives you more control over which apps can access your location data. You can choose to allow apps to access your location all the time, only while you're using the app, or never.

Passkeys: Passkeys are a new type of authentication that is more secure than passwords. Passkeys are unique to each website or app, and they are stored on your device, so they cannot be leaked in a data breach.

2 . New communication features

Live captions for FaceTime calls: This feature automatically captions FaceTime calls in real time. This is helpful for people who are deaf or hard of hearing, and it can also be helpful for people who are in noisy environments.

The ability to collaborate on documents and presentations in Messages: This feature allows you to share documents and presentations with others in Messages, and then collaborate on them in real time. This is a great way to work on projects with friends, family, or colleagues.

3 . New productivity features

Focus Filters: Focus Filters allow you to hide distracting apps and notifications when you're trying to focus on a task. This can help you to be more productive and to get things done more efficiently.

Stage Manager: Stage Manager is a new windowing feature that makes it easier to multitask on iPad. Stage Manager allows you to have multiple windows open at the same time, and you can easily switch between them.

4 . New accessibility features

Live Captions for videos across the system: Live Captions now works for videos across the system, including videos in apps, websites, and social media. This makes it easier for people who are deaf or hard of hearing to enjoy all types of video content.

Door Detection: Door Detection is a new feature that helps blind and low vision users navigate their surroundings. Door Detection uses the LiDAR scanner on iPhone to identify doors, and it provides audio cues to help users find and open them.

In addition to these main advantages, iOS 17 also includes a number of other new features and improvements, such as:

* A redesigned Clock app with new features such as sleep tracking and alarms that wake you up gradually.
* A new Weather app with more detailed weather information and more interactive animations.
* New widgets for the Lock Screen that allow you to see information from your favorite apps at a glance.

Overall, iOS 17 is a significant update that offers a number of new benefits and advantages to users. It is the most secure and privacy-focused version of iOS yet, and it includes a number of new features that can help you to be more productive, communicate more effectively, and get the most out of you

Chapter 1: Getting Started

Set up your iPhone

Here is a more detailed explanation of the steps involved in setting up a new iPhone in iOS 17, with additional information about the new StandBy feature:

1. Turn on your iPhone: When you turn on your iPhone for the first time, you will see the Apple logo. Once the logo disappears, you will see the "Hello" screen.

2. Choose the language and region: On the "Hello" screen, you will be asked to choose the language and region that you want to use. You can also choose to enable VoiceOver, which is a screen reader for people who are blind or have low vision.

3. Connect to a Wi-Fi network: Once you have chosen the language and region, you will be asked to connect to a Wi-Fi network. This is necessary in order to download the latest version of iOS and to set up your Apple ID.

4. Set up Face ID or Touch ID: Face ID and Touch ID are biometric authentication features that allow you to unlock your iPhone and make payments

using your face or fingerprint. To set up Face ID or Touch ID, follow the on-screen instructions.

5. Create a passcode: A passcode is a four-digit or six-digit code that you will need to enter to unlock your iPhone if Face ID or Touch ID is not available. To create a passcode, follow the on-screen instructions.

6. Choose whether or not to transfer data from your previous device: If you have a previous iPhone, you can choose to transfer your data to your new iPhone. To do this, you can use Quick Start, iCloud, or a USB cable.

Note: If you are transferring data from your previous device and you are using iOS 17, you will have the option to transfer your StandBy settings as well. This means that your new iPhone will use the same widgets and brightness settings as your previous iPhone.

7. Set up Apple Pay, if desired: Apple Pay is a mobile payment and digital wallet service that allows you to make payments using your iPhone. To set up Apple Pay, follow the on-screen instructions.

8. Review and accept the terms and conditions: Before you can start using your iPhone, you will need to review and accept the terms and

conditions. To do this, tap "Agree" at the bottom of the screen.

9. Agree to send Apple diagnostic data: Apple collects diagnostic data from its users in order to improve its products and services. To agree to send Apple diagnostic data, tap "Agree" at the bottom of the screen.

10. Create an Apple ID or sign in with your existing Apple ID: An Apple ID is required to use many of the features of your iPhone, such as the App Store, iCloud, and iMessage. If you do not have an Apple ID, you can create one for free. Otherwise, you can sign in with your existing Apple ID.

Once you have completed these steps, your iPhone will be ready to use! You can start exploring the different features and apps that your iPhone has to offer, including the new StandBy feature.

To use StandBy, simply place your iPhone on a charger and turn it on its side: StandBy will automatically turn on and show you a variety of information, including the time, weather, your calendar appointments, notifications, and photos from your library. You can also use StandBy to control your smart home devices.

To customize StandBy, open the Settings app and tap "StandBy": You can choose which widgets to display on StandBy, as well as the brightness of the display.

Learn The Basics Of ios

Learning the basics of iOS is a great way to unlock the full potential of your iPhone or iPad. iOS is a powerful and user-friendly operating system with a wide range of features, so there's something for everyone to enjoy. Here are a few tips for learning the basics of iOS:

- Start with the basics: Before you dive into all the features of iOS, it's important to learn the basics. This includes things like how to navigate the Home screen, how to use the Dock, and how to access the Notification Center and Control Center. You can find this information in the User Guide, which is available on your iPhone or iPad in the Books app.

- Explore the Settings app: The Settings app is where you can customize your iPhone or iPad to your liking. You can change things like the brightness of the screen, the volume of the sound, and the notifications that you receive. You can also use the

Settings app to set up features like Face ID or Touch ID.

- Try out different apps: One of the best ways to learn about iOS is to try out different apps. The App Store is home to millions of apps, so there's something for everyone. Try out different types of apps, such as games, productivity apps, and social media apps.

- Don't be afraid to ask for help: If you're stuck, don't be afraid to ask for help from a friend, family member, or online forum. There are many people who are happy to help new iOS users learn the basics.

- Use Siri: Siri is Apple's voice assistant, and it can be a huge help for learning the basics of iOS. You can use Siri to control your iPhone or iPad with your voice. For example, you can say "Hey Siri, play my favorite song" or "Hey Siri, send a text message to Mom saying I'm on my way home. "

- Take advantage of widgets: Widgets are small interactive panels that can be displayed on the Home screen. They can provide you with quick access to information from different apps, such as the weather, your calendar, or your music library.

- Use the Files app: The Files app is where you can store and manage all of your files on your iPhone or iPad. You can use the Files app to create folders, move files, and share files with other devices.

- Backup your device regularlyIt's important to back up your iPhone or iPad regularly so that you don't lose any important data. You can back up your device to iCloud or to a computer using iTunes or Finder.

Chapter 2: Communication

Phone Calls

Phone calls are a quick and easy way to communicate with others. They can be used for a variety of purposes, such as keeping in touch with friends and family, scheduling appointments, and conducting business. Here are some tips for making and receiving phone calls:

- Be mindful of the time of day when you call. Avoid calling people early in the morning or late at night, unless it is an emergency.
- If you are calling a business, try to call during business hours.
- If you are unable to reach the person you want to speak to, leave a message. Be sure to state your name and number, as well as the reason for your call.
- If you are receiving a call and you are unable to answer it, let the voicemail pick up. You can then listen to the voicemail and return the call later.

Tricks and features of iOS 17 phone calls:

- Live voicemail: Live voicemail allows you to listen to and respond to voicemails in real time, without having to wait for them to finish. To use live voicemail, simply swipe left on the voicemail notification.

- FaceTime video calling for phone calls: You can now start a FaceTime video call directly from a phone call. To do this, tap the FaceTime button in the top right corner of the screen.
- Improved spam filtering: iOS 17 now uses improved machine learning algorithms to filter out spam phone calls. This means that you should receive fewer spam calls overall.
- New call settings: iOS 17 introduces a number of new call settings, such as the ability to silence unknown callers and to block calls from specific numbers.

Additional tricks for using the new phone call features in iOS 17:

- To quickly check your voicemail,, swipe down from the top right corner of the screen and tap the Voicemail icon.
- To start a FaceTime video call from a phone call, tap the FaceTime button in the top right corner of the screen.
- To block calls from a specific number, tap the Info button next to the number in the Phone app, then tap Block This Caller.
- To silence unknown callers, open the Settings app, tap Phone, then tap Silence Unknown Callers.

FaceTime

FaceTime is a video calling app that is built into iOS devices, such as the iPhone, iPad, and Mac. It allows you to make and receive video calls to other FaceTime users.

To make a FaceTime call, you will need the other user's Apple ID. You can either start a FaceTime call from the FaceTime app or from within another app, such as the Phone app or the Messages app.

To start a FaceTime call from the FaceTime app, open the app and tap the "+" button in the top right corner. Then, enter the Apple ID of the person you want to call.

To start a FaceTime call from within another app, tap the FaceTime button next to the person's name.

Once the call is connected, you will be able to see and hear the other person. You can also switch between the front and rear cameras on your device. Here are some of the key features of FaceTime:

- Video calling: FaceTime allows you to make and receive video calls to other FaceTime users.

- Audio calling: FaceTime also allows you to make and receive audio calls to other FaceTime users.
- Group FaceTime: You can make group FaceTime calls with up to 32 people.
- Screen sharing: You can share your screen with other FaceTime users. This is useful for collaborating on projects or giving presentations.
- Live captions: FaceTime can provide live captions for calls. This is useful for people who are deaf or hard of hearing.

Some Additional Tips For Using Facetime:

Make sure that you have a good internet connection. FaceTime calls require a strong internet connection in order to work well.
* Use a headset or earbuds. This will improve the audio quality of your calls.
* Adjust the lighting. Make sure that you are in a well-lit area so that the other person can see you clearly.
* Be mindful of your background. Try to find a quiet place with a neutral background for your calls.

FaceTime is a great way to stay connected with friends and family, and to collaborate with colleagues. By following these tips, you can get the most out of FaceTime.

Messages

Messages is a messaging app that is built into iOS devices, such as the iPhone, iPad, and Mac. It allows you to send and receive text messages, images, videos, and other types of files.

Messages is a popular communication tool for people of all ages. It is used for a variety of purposes, such as staying in touch with friends and family, coordinating plans, and sharing information.

Here are some of the key features of Messages in the aspect of communication:

- End-to-end encryption: Messages uses end-to-end encryption to protect your privacy. This means that only you and the person you are communicating with can read or hear your messages.
- iMessage: iMessage is a messaging service that is built into Messages. It allows you to send and receive messages to other Apple users for free.
- Group messaging: Messages allows you to create group chats with up to 25 people. This is a great way to stay in touch with multiple people at once.
- Audio messages: Messages allows you to send and receive audio messages. This is

a convenient way to communicate if you do not have time to type a message.

- Stickers and animations: Messages includes a variety of stickers and animations that you can use to add personality to your messages.
- Read receipts and typing indicators: Messages lets you know when the other person has read your message and when they are typing a response. This can be helpful for knowing when to expect a response.

Mail

Mail is an email app that is built into iOS devices, such as the iPhone, iPad, and Mac. It allows you to send and receive emails from a variety of email providers, such as Gmail, Outlook, and Yahoo.

Mail is a popular communication tool for people of all ages. It is used for a variety of purposes, such as staying in touch with friends and family, conducting business, and receiving news and updates.

Here are some of the key features of Mail in the aspect of communication:

- Email filtering: Mail allows you to filter your emails so that you can quickly find the ones you are looking for. You can filter emails by sender, recipient, subject, and other criteria.

- Smart mailboxes: Mail creates smart mailboxes for you, such as unread emails, starred emails, and important emails. This makes it easy to keep track of your emails and to find the ones you need quickly.
- Search: Mail has a powerful search feature that allows you to find any email in your inbox. You can search by sender, recipient, subject, body, and other criteria.
- Attachments: Mail allows you to send and receive email attachments, such as photos, videos, and documents.
- Flagging and starring: Mail allows you to flag and star emails so that you can easily follow up on them later.

Here are some additional tips for using Mail to communicate effectively:

* Use a clear and concise subject line for your emails. This will help the recipient to understand what the email is about and whether or not it is important.
* Be clear and concise in the body of your emails. Avoid using jargon or technical terms that the recipient may not understand.
* Proofread your emails before you send them.
* Use a professional email address and signature.

* Be mindful of the time of day when you send emails. Avoid sending emails early in the morning or late at night, unless it is an emergency.

Mail is a powerful communication tool that can be used to stay in touch with others, conduct business, and receive news and updates. By following these tips, you can get the most out of Mail and communicate effectively with others.

Chapter 3: Photos and Camera

Take photos and videos

The iOS 17 Photos and Camera apps include a number of new features that make it easier and more fun to take and manage your photos and videos. Here are some of the most notable new features:

Camera

Improved low-light performance: The camera on iOS 17 has improved low-light performance, so you can take better photos and videos in dark conditions.

New cinematic mode effects: Cinematic mode now supports more effects, such as Portrait Cinematic mode, which allows you to blur the background in videos of people.

New macro mode for the front-facing camera: The front-facing camera now has a macro mode, so you can take close-up photos and videos of small objects.

New level indicator: The camera now has a level indicator to help you take straight photos and videos.

Photos

New Live Text features: Live Text can now recognize and extract text from videos, and you can translate text directly from photos and videos.

New Visual Look Up features: Visual Look Up can now identify plants, animals, and landmarks in photos and videos, and you can get more information about them by tapping and holding on them.

New Shared Library: The Shared Library is a new way to share photos and videos with friends and family. You can create a shared library with up to five other people, and everyone in the library can add, edit, and delete photos and videos.

New Memories features: Memories now includes more music options, and you can create Memories from specific dates or locations.

In addition to these new features, iOS 17 also includes a number of other improvements to the Photos and Camera apps, such as faster performance and a more intuitive interface.

Here are some tips for using the new features in the iOS 17 Photos and Camera apps:

Camera

* To use the improved low-light performance, tap the Night mode button in the upper left corner of the screen when you're taking a photo or video in low light.
* To use the new cinematic mode effects, tap the Cinematic button in the lower left corner of the screen when you're recording a video.
* To use the new macro mode for the front-facing camera, tap the Macro button in the lower left corner of the screen when you're taking a photo or video.
* To use the new level indicator, look for the white line in the middle of the screen. If the line is not level, tilt your phone or iPad until it is.

Photos

* To use the new Live Text features, tap the Live Text button in the lower right corner of the screen.
* To use the new Visual Look Up features, tap and hold on any text or object in a photo or video.
* To create a Shared Library, go to the Shared Libraries tab in the Photos app and tap Create New Shared Library.
* To create a Memory from a specific date or location, go to the Memories tab in the Photos app and tap the + button. Then, tap Create Memory and select the date or location you want to use.

Edit Photos And Videos

The iOS 17 Photos and Camera apps have introduced several exciting new editing features to enhance your photo and video editing capabilities. These features make it easier and more powerful to edit your photos and videos directly on your iPhone or iPad. Here's a breakdown of the key editing features and some tips on how to use them:

Photo Editing:

New One-Tap Adjustments: iOS 17 now offers one-tap adjustments like Auto Enhance, Auto Contrast, and Auto White Balance. These quick adjustments can instantly improve the overall quality of your photos. To use them, tap the Edit button in the top right corner of the screen, then tap the Auto button.

New Curves Tool: The curves tool is a powerful addition that allows you to fine-tune the brightness, contrast, and saturation of your photos. To access it, tap the Edit button, then tap Adjust, and finally, tap the Curves icon.

New Selective Adjustments: You can now make selective adjustments to specific areas of your photos. For instance, you can adjust the brightness, contrast, or saturation of a specific object or part of the photo. To use this feature, tap

Edit, then Select, and choose the area you want to edit.

New Masking Tools: The masking tools enable you to select specific areas of a photo to edit while leaving the rest of the image untouched. This feature allows for precise edits to specific parts of your photo. To use the masking tools, tap Edit, then Tools, and finally, tap the Mask icon.

Video Editing:

New Multi-Clip Editing: iOS 17 introduces the ability to edit multiple video clips together into a single video project. To start multi-clip editing, tap the + button in the bottom left corner of the screen and select the clips you want to include in your project.

New Precision Trimming: With precision trimming, you can trim your videos with greater accuracy, down to the frame level. Tap the Trim button in the bottom right corner of the screen, and then drag the sliders to make precise trims to your video.

New Effects and Transitions: iOS 17 provides a variety of new effects and transitions to enhance your videos. To add these effects and transitions, tap the Effects button in the bottom right corner of the screen, and select the ones you want to apply to your video.

New Color Grading Tools: Color grading tools allow you to adjust the color, contrast, and saturation of your videos, giving you more control over the visual style of your content. Access these tools by tapping the Color button in the bottom right corner and adjusting the sliders as needed.

These new editing features in iOS 17 are designed to offer more creative freedom and control over your photos and videos directly on your iOS device. Experiment with these tools to enhance your content and create stunning visuals with ease.

Share Photos And Videos

The iOS 17 Photos and Camera apps have introduced a range of new sharing features that significantly enhance the way you can share your photos and videos with others. These features are designed to offer more convenience, flexibility, and collaboration options. Here's an expanded explanation of these new sharing features:

New Messages Integration:

With the integration of Messages, sharing photos and videos has become even more straightforward. You can now directly share your media content with your contacts through Messages. Simply open the photo or video you want to share, tap the Share button, select Messages, and choose the conversation where you want to send it. This seamless integration streamlines the sharing process, making it easier to communicate visually.

New AirDrop Enhancements:

AirDrop, Apple's file-sharing feature, has received enhancements in iOS 17. You can now share photos and videos with multiple recipients simultaneously via AirDrop. To use this feature, open the photo or video, tap the Share button, then tap the AirDrop button, and select all the recipients you want to share the content with. This makes sharing moments with friends and family more efficient and enjoyable.

New Shared Libraries:

Shared libraries offer a fresh way to collaborate on photos and videos with your loved ones. You can create a shared library that includes up to five other people, and everyone in the library has the ability to add, edit, and delete photos and videos. This collaborative approach ensures that everyone can contribute to and enjoy shared memories. To create a shared library, navigate to the Shared Libraries tab in the Photos app and tap "Create New Shared Library. "

New iCloud Photos Features:

iCloud Photos has gained new features to enhance your photo and video sharing experiences. You can now share individual photos and videos directly from your iCloud Photos library with others. Additionally, you have the option to create shared albums that allow for collaborative curation and sharing. To share a specific photo or video from iCloud Photos, open the item, tap the Share button, select iCloud Photos, and choose "Share Link. " To create a shared album, visit the Albums tab in the Photos app, tap the + button, and select "Create Shared Album. "

These sharing features not only simplify the sharing process but also promote collaboration and interaction among friends and family. Whether you're instantly sharing a moment through Messages, efficiently distributing media via AirDrop, collaborating in shared libraries, or curating albums in iCloud Photos, iOS 17 offers a suite of tools to enhance your digital sharing experiences. With faster performance and a user-friendly interface, iOS 17 ensures that your memories are easily accessible and enjoyable to share.

Chapter 4: iCloud

IOS 17 upgrades for icloud

New Shared Libraries:
Shared libraries in iOS 17 provide a fantastic way to share your precious photos and videos with friends and family in a more collaborative and interactive manner. Here's a deeper look at how shared libraries work:

Creation: To create a shared library, head to the "Shared Libraries" tab within the Photos app. Once there, tap on "Create New Shared Library. " This action will initiate the process of setting up a shared space for your chosen content.

Adding Members: After initiating the creation of a shared library, you can start adding the people you want to share this library with. Invite friends or family members to join this collaborative space where everyone can contribute and enjoy shared photos and videos.

Collaboration: Once you've set up a shared library and added members, everyone in the library gains the ability to actively participate. They can add their own photos and videos, edit existing content, or even delete items as needed. This collaborative approach ensures that everyone can contribute to and enjoy shared memories, making it ideal for events like family gatherings, vacations, or special occasions.

Enhanced Sharing: Shared libraries provide an enriched way of sharing memories. It's perfect for creating shared albums of a family vacation, allowing multiple contributors to capture different perspectives and moments. As everyone in the library has editing privileges, it's easy to curate a collection of memorable photos and videos.

Improved Family Sharing:

iOS 17 also brings enhancements to Family Sharing, which allows family members to share various Apple services. Here's a closer look:

iCloud+ Sharing: With iOS 17, Family Sharing can now extend to iCloud+ storage. You can share your iCloud+ subscription with up to five family members, enabling them to enjoy the benefits of iCloud+ storage, including expanded storage space and enhanced privacy features like iCloud Private Relay and Hide My Email.

Setup: To start Family Sharing, navigate to the Settings app, tap your name, and then select "Family Sharing. " Follow the prompts to set up Family Sharing and share iCloud+ storage and subscription benefits with your loved ones. This feature can lead to cost savings on iCloud+ subscriptions for your family.

New iCloud Settings:
iOS 17 introduces a set of new and useful iCloud settings that provide more control over your iCloud data and storage. Here's what you can do with these settings:

App Data Backup Control: You now have the ability to select which apps can back up their data to iCloud. This feature allows you to fine-tune your iCloud backups by including or excluding specific apps, helping you manage your iCloud storage more efficiently.

Mass iCloud Data Deletion: iOS 17 offers the option to delete iCloud data from all of your devices simultaneously. This streamlined approach simplifies data management across your Apple ecosystem, ensuring that unwanted data is removed consistently from all connected devices.

Tips for Utilizing These Features:

Collaborative Photo Projects: Utilize shared libraries for collaborative photo projects or albums, such as documenting a family vacation, birthday celebration, or a special event where multiple contributors can share their perspectives.

Cost-Efficient iCloud+ Sharing: Leverage Family Sharing to share iCloud+ storage and its benefits with your family members. This can lead to cost savings on iCloud subscriptions while providing everyone with ample storage space.

Customize iCloud Backups: Use the new iCloud settings to tailor your iCloud backups by selecting specific apps to include or exclude from backup. This customization helps you manage your iCloud storage effectively.

Streamlined Data Management: Take advantage of the ability to delete iCloud data from all your devices simultaneously. This feature simplifies data management and ensures consistent data removal.

In summary, iOS 17's new iCloud features significantly enhance your ability to share, collaborate, and manage your photos, videos, and iCloud services. Whether you're collaborating on family memories, optimizing iCloud storage, or fine-tuning your data backups, these features provide greater flexibility and control over your digital experiences.

Chapter 5: Accessibility

Accessibility Features On Iphone

iCloud Accessibility features are a vital set of tools designed to enhance the usability of iPhone devices for individuals with disabilities. These features can be easily enabled through the Settings app, specifically under "Accessibility > Accessibility Features. " Let's explore some of the essential iCloud Accessibility features available on your iPhone:

VoiceOver: VoiceOver serves as a screen reader that audibly narrates everything displayed on your iPhone screen. This includes reading out text, labels, buttons, and various screen elements. VoiceOver empowers users with visual impairments to navigate and interact with their device.

Zoom: The Zoom feature allows you to magnify the entire screen or a specific portion of it. This can be particularly helpful for individuals with low vision, enabling them to see content more clearly.

Screen Curtain: Screen Curtain is a feature that hides the visual content on the screen, allowing users to concentrate solely on audio output. It can be invaluable for those who rely on voice guidance and auditory feedback.

Guided Access: Guided Access offers the ability to restrict iPhone access to a specific app or a designated portion of the screen. This feature is beneficial for individuals with attention deficit hyperactivity disorder (ADHD) or autism spectrum disorder (ASD) who may require a focused and distraction-free environment.

Accessibility Shortcuts: Accessibility Shortcuts provide a quick and convenient way to enable or disable Accessibility features with a simple triple-click of the side or Home button. This shortcut streamlines the process of activating these essential features.

iCloud Accessibility Feature Benefits:
One significant advantage of iCloud Accessibility features is that they are stored in your iCloud account. This means you can access and utilize these features seamlessly across all your Apple devices, including your iPhone, iPad, and Mac. This unified experience ensures consistency and convenience in using your devices to accommodate your accessibility needs.

Tips for Utilizing iCloud Accessibility Features on iPhone:
Here are some helpful tips for effectively using iCloud Accessibility features on your iPhone:

Enabling VoiceOver: To activate VoiceOver, navigate to "Settings > Accessibility > Accessibility Features > VoiceOver" and toggle the switch to enable it.

Enabling Zoom: To utilize Zoom, go to "Settings > Accessibility > Accessibility Features > Zoom" and switch it on.

Enabling Screen Curtain: To hide your screen content with Screen Curtain, access "Settings > Accessibility > Accessibility Features > Screen Curtain" and turn it on.

Enabling Guided Access: To set up Guided Access, visit "Settings > Accessibility > Accessibility Features > Guided Access" and enable it.

Adding Accessibility Shortcuts: To create an Accessibility Shortcut, visit "Settings > Accessibility > Accessibility Features > Accessibility Shortcuts" and tap "Add New Shortcut. " Customize your shortcuts to suit your preferences.

In conclusion, iCloud Accessibility features empower individuals with disabilities to use their iPhone devices with greater ease and efficiency. Whether you require screen reading, magnification, focused app usage, or quick accessibility shortcuts, these features are thoughtfully designed to enhance your iPhone experience and improve accessibility across your Apple ecosystem.

Turn on accessibility features

To turn on accessibility features on your device, you will need to go to the settings menu. The specific steps involved will vary depending on the device you are using, but here are some general guidelines:

- Open the Settings app.
- Tap or click on Accessibility.
- On some devices, you may need to tap or click on Advanced to see all of the accessibility features.
- Browse through the list of accessibility features and find the ones that you want to enable.
- Tap or click the toggle switch next to each feature to turn it on.

Chapter 6 : Troubleshooting

iOS 17 introduces a range of powerful troubleshooting features to assist users in diagnosing and resolving issues with their devices. These features are designed to enhance the overall user experience by offering quick and effective solutions. Here's an in-depth look at these troubleshooting features and common problems users may encounter with their iOS devices, along with their respective solutions:

1. System Diagnostics:
System Diagnostics provides users with a comprehensive overview of their device's health.
It offers insights into battery health, storage status, and network connectivity.
Various diagnostic tests are available to identify specific issues, such as performance or connectivity problems.

2. Guided Troubleshooting:
Guided Troubleshooting offers step-by-step instructions to help users resolve common device-related problems.
For instance, if you're facing Wi-Fi connectivity issues, this feature will guide you through the troubleshooting steps.

3. Recovery Mode Assistant:
The Recovery Mode Assistant simplifies the process of recovering your device from Recovery Mode.

If your device becomes stuck in Recovery Mode, this assistant provides clear instructions for restoring your device or updating to the latest iOS version.

In addition to these new troubleshooting features, iOS 17 also improves existing tools like the Activity Monitor and Crash Logs, making it easier for users to diagnose and resolve issues.

Common Problems and Solutions:

Problem: Your device is running slowly.
Solution:Restart your device, which can often resolve minor performance issues.

Close unused apps running in the background to free up system resources.

Check for software updates; Apple frequently releases updates with performance improvements.

Delete unused apps and files to free up storage space.

As a last resort, consider resetting your device to factory settings, which can resolve persistent performance problems.

Problem: Your device is not connecting to Wi-Fi.
Solution:

Restart your router and modem; this can resolve minor connectivity issues.

Ensure you enter the correct Wi-Fi password when connecting to your network.

Try connecting to a different Wi-Fi network to isolate the problem.

Reset your network settings (note that this will erase saved networks and passwords).

Update your router's firmware; this may fix certain Wi-Fi connectivity issues.

Problem: Your device is not charging.
Solution:Test with a different charging cable; a damaged cable can be the issue.

Attempt to charge from another power outlet to rule out a faulty outlet.

Clean the device's charging port; dust or dirt may hinder the connection.

Restart your device, which can resolve minor charging problems.

As a last resort, consider restoring your device to factory settings to address persistent charging issues.

If you've attempted these troubleshooting steps and continue to experience problems with your iOS device, don't hesitate to contact Apple Support for further assistance. These comprehensive troubleshooting features in iOS 17 aim to empower users to resolve issues effectively and enjoy a smoother user experience.

Get Support From Apple

If you encounter any problems or issues with iOS 17, Apple offers several avenues for getting the support you need to resolve them effectively:

1. Visit the Apple Support Website:
The Apple Support website is a valuable resource for troubleshooting common iOS device issues.
You can search for specific problems or explore a wide range of topics to find relevant information and solutions.

2. Contact Apple Support by Phone:
If you're unable to resolve your issue using the online resources, you can reach out to Apple Support by phone.

Apple Support representatives are available around the clock, 24/7, to assist you with your concerns.

3. Visit an Apple Store:

If you have an Apple Store nearby, consider visiting in person for hands-on support.
Apple Store staff can help diagnose and troubleshoot your issue, providing on-the-spot solutions.

Tips for Effective Apple Support:

Provide Device Information: When seeking support, be prepared to share information about your device and describe the problem you're experiencing. This will assist Apple Support representatives in diagnosing and addressing the issue promptly.

Be Patient and Polite: Remember that Apple Support representatives are there to assist you, so maintain patience and politeness during interactions.

Follow Instructions: If an Apple Support representative provides instructions or troubleshooting steps, follow them carefully to expedite the resolution process and increase the likelihood of a successful outcome.

If you're facing any challenges with iOS 17, don't hesitate to reach out to Apple Support. Their trained professionals are equipped to help you navigate and troubleshoot problems, ensuring you can make the most of your iOS experience.

Features and tricks

iOS 17 is a major update to Apple's mobile operating system, and it includes a number of new features and tricks. Here are some of the most notable:

New lock screen customization options:iOS 17 allows you to customize the look and feel of your lock screen more than ever before. You can change the font and color of the date and time, add widgets, and even use a video as your wallpaper.

Interactive widgets: iOS 17 widgets are now interactive, meaning you can perform actions directly from the home screen. For example, you can tap on a music widget to play a song or tap on a weather widget to see the forecast.

Focus filters: Focus filters allow you to hide distracting content from apps while you're working on a specific task. For example, you could create a Focus filter for work that hides all of your social media apps.

Live Text improvements: Live Text is now even more powerful, allowing you to interact with text in images and videos. For example, you can translate text in real time or copy and paste text from images and videos.

Shared iCloud Photo Library: iOS 17 makes it easy to share your photos with family and friends with the new Shared iCloud Photo Library. You can choose which photos to share and give others permission to add, edit, and delete photos from the shared library.

New Messages features: iOS 17 includes a number of new Messages features, such as the ability to edit or unsend messages, mark messages as unread, and collaborate on projects with others.

New Mail features: iOS 17 also includes a number of new Mail features, such as the ability to schedule emails, undo send, and receive reminders about emails.

Here are some tricks for using iOS 17:

Use quick actions to launch apps and perform tasks. Quick actions are shortcuts to frequently used apps and tasks that you can access from the home screen or lock screen. To create a quick action, long-press on an app icon and tap on "Customize Activity. "

Use Siri to control your device and perform tasks. Siri is Apple's voice assistant, and it can be used to control your device and perform tasks without having to lift a finger. To activate Siri, say "Hey Siri" or hold down the side button on your device.

Use keyboard shortcuts to navigate your device and perform tasks. iOS 17 includes a number of keyboard shortcuts that can help you navigate your device and perform tasks more quickly. To see a list of all available keyboard shortcuts, open the Settings app and go to "General" > "Keyboard" > "Keyboard Shortcuts. "

Use AssistiveTouch to access features and perform tasks without having to tap the screen. AssistiveTouch is a feature that allows you to access features and perform tasks without having to tap the screen. To enable AssistiveTouch, open the Settings app and go to "Accessibility" > "Touch" > "AssistiveTouch. "

These are just a few of the many new features and tricks in iOS 17. Be sure to explore the operating system and discover all that it has to offer.

iOS 17 specifications

iOS 17 is the seventeenth major release of Apple's iOS operating system for the iPhone and the successor to iOS 16. It was announced on June 5, 2023, at Apple's annual Worldwide Developers Conference, and released publicly on September 18, 2023.

Here are some of the specifications of iOS 17:

1 . Supported devices: iPhone XR/iPhone XS and later, which means it drops support for the iPhone 8, iPhone 8 Plus, and iPhone X.

2 . New features:
- New lock screen customization options
- Interactive widgets
- Focus filters
- Live Text improvements
- Shared iCloud Photo Library
- New Messages features
- New Mail features

3 . Other improvements:
- General performance and stability improvements
- Improved security and privacy features
- New accessibility features

To install iOS 17, you can go to the Settings app and tap on "General" > "Software Update." If iOS 17 is available, you will see a notification. Tap on "Download and Install" to install the update.

CONCLUSION

In conclusion, iOS 17 brings a wealth of new features, enhancements, and accessibility options to Apple's mobile devices, making them more versatile, user-friendly, and powerful than ever before. This user guide has provided an extensive overview of the key highlights in iOS 17, from its new features like StandBy, Live Activities, and Visual Look Up to improved functionalities in photo and video editing, sharing, and accessibility.

Additionally, we explored the benefits of iCloud Accessibility features, which empower individuals with disabilities to navigate and utilize their iPhone devices effectively. These features, including VoiceOver, Zoom, Screen Curtain, Guided Access, and Accessibility Shortcuts, ensure that everyone can enjoy the iOS experience.

iOS 17 also introduces troubleshooting features like System Diagnostics, Guided Troubleshooting, and Recovery Mode Assistant, which empower users to identify and resolve device issues more efficiently. Common problems, such as slow performance, Wi-Fi connectivity, and charging, were discussed along with recommended solutions.

For users facing more challenging issues, the user guide offered guidance on seeking support from Apple. Whether through the Apple Support website, phone support, or visiting an Apple Store, users have access to a range of resources and experts ready to assist.

In summary, iOS 17 is a significant milestone in the ongoing evolution of Apple's mobile operating system. With its innovative features, enhanced accessibility, troubleshooting capabilities, and robust support options, iOS 17 continues to elevate the user experience and ensure that Apple devices remain reliable and enjoyable tools for people of all backgrounds and abilities. As you explore iOS 17 on your iPhone or iPad, we encourage you to make the most of these features and seek assistance when needed to fully embrace the potential of your Apple device.